D0556805

73

38 Bar Blues
a collection of poetry

ᘓ

by C. R. Avery

Write Bloody Publishing
America's Independent Press

Long Beach, CA

WRITEBLOODY.COM

Avery, C.R..
2ⁿᵈ edition.
ISBN: 978-1-935904-08-3

Interior Layout by Lea C. Deschenes
Cover Designed by Joshua Grieve
Cover Art by C. R. Avery
Proofread by Sarah Kay
Edited by Write Bloody Publishing Editorial Staff
Type set in Bergamo: www.theleagueofmoveabletype.com

Printed in Tennessee, USA

Write Bloody Publishing
Long Beach, CA
Support Independent Presses
writebloody.com

To contact the author, send an email to writebloody@gmail.com

38 Bar Blues

CHAPTER FOUR
A DRAGON, WITH HIS TAIL
CURLED UP LIKE A GARDEN HOSE

CHAPTER ONE
CHERRY BLOSSOM GRAVEYARD

Les Deux Saints de Montreal

Her black bra is on the dresser,
wool hand-me-down coat on my back.
St. Lawrence prays for a confessor,
St. Catherine begs to differ and leads the attack.

The army of migrant workers are ready.
"No devil in Montreal!"
The snow was fast and steady,
each motel watched it fall.

Sheltered in the basement of her computer house,
under the surveillance of a high-end store,
edge of Chinatown, quiet as a church mouse,
I pray for St. Lawrence, St. Catherine, and migrants of the war.

A Few Thousand Words

The sun has gone to sleep in a heap of summer dresses.
The Mexican moon has not risen from her foldout bed
for the 9 below zero night shift.
Please lift the lights in the apartment windows of our village.
They are our only lonely guide
through the charcoal cold of her bitchy mysteries.
They will shine and illuminate unshaven black thighs
up to her royal blue undergarments,
waiting for handsome altar boys who are really young dykes
with switch blades concealed under their cloaks
to light the orphan stars.

Smoke by your train soaked window.
My art history class was drawing female nudes
that would have given Picasso a hard-on
and make Big Mama Thornton's cootchie wet.

While bathing in semi-expensive red wine,
we all took turns as model and observer.
One stripped slowly with red cheeks,
the other returned from the washroom wearing nothing but a bowler hat.
Both beautiful like a Coney Island Ferris wheel,
adorable like foxes in the chicken coop.
Have you ever seen a hobo naked?
He looks like a millionaire.

From the 4th floor balcony,
a disfigured cat growls in a car-width wide alleyway below,
by the light blue "smells like teen spirit" dumpster,
a dirty rose in its yellow teeth and soon in its hungry belly,
while the big-breasted moon climbs the stairs to her post.

She casually smiles in the modern world darkness,
taking the universe by storm.

Now the women are clothed and silent in separate rooms
while the man pounds on a typewriter on the fire escape
like Father Time.
Sadly, the sketching class is no longer oil based and naked
in a 3 penny pencil drawing opera
of see-through apron excitement.

But look out your train soaked window.
You can read about a period in art history
that undressed by lamp light,
right here in our tiny village.

Man Sitting Beside Me at a Campfire

I asked him if he was a musician;
he said, "No,"
but added, "I write some poetry, though."
Later in the evening
I asked when he started writing.
He replied, "When my wife left me,"
then looked into the fire as it crackled and warmed us in the rain
and added,
"It was also around the same time
I started hanging out with criminals."

ARCTIC WIND

My woman has a tattoo on her back
no one sees.

It only appears when my hand glides down from the bottom of her neck
to the imprint on her skin of a tightly-worn belt.
It's fine-line detailed, giant monarch butterfly wings.

As we make love, they flap like a helicopter propeller,
fanning our bodies like arctic wind,
or an open ice box.

As we lie in bed after kissing the inside of earlobes
with alarm clock's radio,
moonshine bottle dry,
smoking satisfied,
I watch the ink run
all Halloween orange
and black licorice blue,
dripping down to her sweet ass
which of course I squeeze,
her wings now hidden from the world.

BIRD CAGE

She had an old barrelhouse upright,
what piano tuners call a bird cage.
They're too old to fix,
beyond repair,
are only useful to tone deaf fugitives
or as muted decoration.

There are always many trinkets on these barrelhouse birdcages:
pictures in frames,
some loose,
a jar of pennies,
junk mail,
little ceramic animals,
and a light coat of dust on the piano's driveway.

The lid is always down,
so the black and white keys
are sleeping like little girl dolls
under wooden blankets.

I'm in my toque and scarf,
staring at this musical family heirloom.
"Do you know how to orchestrate such a contraption?" she asks.
"Not very well," I reply.
"I can bang out a few chords, but no ragtime rabbit-out-of-the-hat tricks."

Almost like she was a man
who just helped his buddy move,
or who had just mowed many miles of lawns,
or like she was Stanley Kowalski in A Streetcar Named Desire,
she nonchalantly removes her shirt
in this living of living rooms
of old furniture
and a unique antique lamp
(with which my suitcase is trying to have a big discussion about
    Hunter S. Thompson
but the lamp's not having it.)

The lamp is transfixed on her,
she can even turn on the lamp.

As she sits on the couch beside me,
her naked back against the side armrest,
she stretches out her crickety bridge legs
on top of my rushing river lap,
flowing dangerous below her haunted legs.
The objects in my pocket have already turned to stone.

"How have your travels been?" she asks while getting cozy.
"I saw Nelson Mandela speak in Trafalgar Square."
"How was that?"
"Well, there were many birds flying overhead
before, during, and after he spoke."
"What did he talk about?"
This is the question that leaves me breathless.
I stare down at my old Adidas,
my hands turn into cranes
picking her bridging the gap legs
off my flowing into Lake Ontario lap.
I walk over to the piano
as my shoes give weight
and she watches in opera house quiet.

I sit down at the circle-rotating stool,
lift up its lid
in the bottom register
just below middle C,
my right hand turns into an ignition
receiving the key.

"What's this got to do with Nelson Mandela?"
"His son just died of AIDS and I'm trying to remember this funeral
    march I know."

Birds,
thousands of birds,
fly out from the barrelhouse piano's cage,
flap around the room and out the window.

She skates across the room,
leans in,
places her palm on the outside of my pocket,
feeling the outline of the stone.
"What's this?" she asks.
"Oh, that's my magic hour sailor song."
Her eyebrow goes up in a triangle
expressing, "don't be pullin' my bridge."
I explain,
"Each night at dusk
when it's too early to sleep
and too dark to look for food,
we sing
in a repetitive rhythmic chirping
that pierces the spirit with bad-ass fuckin' blues."
She pulls out the harmonica from the river's mud,
puts it to my teeth,
and whispers,
"Smooth as a stone, play free as a migrating bird:
one who's been banned from religion
like love and the f-word."

So each night I do it for her,
just so she knows that whatever happens,
this world will not make muted decoration out of me.

Across the room, my suitcase is screaming at that antique lamp,
"So what, I was born to wander, you're easily unplugged!
And fugitives are free."

She had an old barrelhouse upright,
what piano tuners call
a birdcage.

My 'What Next' Memo to Myself

I wore a leather tie
and a yellow shirt with paint stains,
half-covered by a black suit jacket.

I didn't have a ticket and I didn't have a date
and I walked to my high school prom.
Straight down Rideau Street to the Château Laurier,
a flask of Southern Comfort in my inside coat pocket,
with it half empty and the prom half over,
showed up at the fancy shindig hotel.

It looked like a crystal fuckin' palace,
and I was smack-dab in the middle of the be-all, end-all ball.

Passed the French teacher who saw me come in;
he knew I was drunk.
He also knew I hadn't bought a ticket.
"Can't do what ten people tell me to do,"
whispers Otis to Wilson Picket.

I danced with a couple of girls,
but their eyes were bugged out
like they had just seen a ghost.
Maybe it was because of the incredible stiff erection I had while we danced.
Sorry, ladies,
I knew the bell tolled for me.

From there to a few boring-as-all-hell hotel rooms
with odd numbers of kids drinking or passed out,
so with a free taxi voucher
the heads of the prom committee were givin' away
like 1-800 pizza delivery flyers,
I took a cab home.

Was livin' in a house with a few other high school students,
none that I hung with,
but for a hundred bucks I rented a large closet under the stairs
which smelled like wet dreams and bad poetry.

I took off my tie and yellow shirt,
stayed up all night at my little desk
writing my thesis,
my 'what next' memo to myself.

As the sun came up like a cheap diner breakfast
or a trumpet practicing its scales,
I packed my travelin' bag with books and clothes,
left the rest behind and left for good.
Headed to the 401 highway and hitchhiked East
on route to Newfoundland,
hoping for a gig at the Fat Cat Blues Bar in St. John's.

Smoking that evening under the motion detector porch light
of a closed auto shop
somewhere in Quebec,
an hour or so outside its capital city,
taking in each puff,
watching the smoke curl in the light,
it tasted like victory.
Yes, ladies,
it tolled for me.

ATTENDANT

I'm petrified.
Lately I've been workin' at Jonathan's Exotic Roadside,
a gas station by the Triple A hockey stadium parking lot
on First and Floozy Boulevard. It's a full service spot.
You can self-serve if you want,
to me it doesn't really matter,
but for the extra nickel I'll fill ya up
and clean yer windshield from suicide bomber bug splatter.

Customers pay inside Jonathan's Exotic,
so I don't have to deal with the money headache;
just fast, furious, and efficient,
sunrise to sundown
with a twenty-minute lunch break.

I usually buy it,
Pepsi and a Jos. Louis
are my low-carb diet.
That way I'm more Marlon Brando
than I'll ever be James Dean.
The convenience of this gas station cuisine.

When I get home a woman in her underwear greets me
with a hand grenade and a bar of soap.
I've been choosing the latter as of late,
heading straight
to the shower
to wash the slime from my fingernails
and grime from my hair
from dirty headlights.
I walk into the bedroom in a towel,
to the hum of a small fan
blowing over our chocolate cake quiet nights
of homemade love making.
I mean, we keep things interesting,
but it's not a perve she kiss
but I wake up with these cars to service.

Music floats out of the automobiles
like the aroma of burnt toast.
It's the secret strength
of the concrete jungle compost,
but when they turn off their engines,
the music comes to a complete stop.
The kids and the family dog
stare out from the back seat,
and my momentum does drop
like the middle of any biblical fable.

Today I walked over to the picnic table,
lit a smoke,
thinking my life in the arts
has made me a gas attendant
on First and Floozy Boulevard.
Just waiting for a sign,
for God to play his wild card.
And these Jonathan's Exotic Roadside visions
are simple and obvious
as when a woman removes her street clothes
and gives you that all-knowing glance,
you know that it's time
to take off your pants.
You know what I'm saying?

I knew the keys were still in the ignition
'cause the music was still playing,
just because some random soul
with good enough intentions
went in to pay for his fuel.
Maybe modest in his musical taste,
as the radio played the regular rotation of another pop song ...
                    the regular rotation of another pop song ...
                        the regular rotation of another pop song ...

but I didn't miss the opportunity.
Free as the early bird worm in the mouth of the moon
as it reflected in the blue Chrysler's rear view mirror,
I climbed inside and drove away—

not a thief,
not a musician,
not a poet with something to say,
just a gas attendant who knew the time was right
to blow up a spot,
show the little girls and boys how it's done.

It's not a matter of picking straws,
it was by outlaws the West was won.
Found a classical music station on the radio,
turned it up real loud,
ate my Jos. Louis
as the violins swelled,
the vision seemed to crescendo while they played.

Baby, tonight
I'll be using that hand grenade.
The truth is,
we're all petrified,
but when the opportunity arises, kid,
don't be denied.

LIKE THAT PAINTING IN HIGH SCHOOL

Hemingway wrote, "Othello was a nigger."
Kerouac tripped over "faggot"
and other character-defining
dated slurs in his books.

Yes, of course, both these men had enough humanity to be redeemed
but being a product of popular vote,
what phrases and broken words have I written
that will give the firing squad a scapegoat?

Perpetuating stupidity instead of eradicating it,
sentences that will show holes in my old uniform's game,
outlining my shortcomings with white chalk,
bringing to light its ignorant and sheltered dead pan.

There's the misplacement blues of being ahead of your time,
but the same spider weaves the web of playing to your crowd for an
        easy laugh.

I hold on to the cool metal pole
and stare out at blurry French graffiti
through the window of no compromise's fast moving train
on a purgatory two zone metro pass,
my lips dry as a genocide
with each possible careless murmur
that my pen and I decide
to carve into an old oak tree.
Remembering what was considered acceptable in 1953
has not stood the test of time.

Eddie Murphy now
still sounds raw,
but a little homophobic
in a red leather suit,
stepping on a widow spider.

St. Marie

Start spreading the news
soft cues
can be heard
as pigeons flap their wings
and the church cock ah doo's
its bells at high noon
castle sand dunes down below
under forty year-old snow
people walk in preoccupied circumstance
modern dance shuffle
while a chocolate rosemary truffle
is in the clutch of an old Italian hobbit woman
who immigrated from Sicily in 1912
looks up from bended knees folded like linen
to mother Mary
while an ordinary
subway car untagged
carries the news of speed
like Lightning speaks of Hopkins electricity
like T.V. speaks in volumes
in the coffee houses
the infidels
after church bells of holy trinity
speak of St. Marie.

A hustle is a hustle stupid
tin pan alley cupid
clothes pin in the side of smooth
tattooed on your memory like Scooby Doo
after running off the yellow school bus
revolution in a French fairy tale
computer in a Spanish folk song
the memos went out
notifying the proper authorities
that people would be in fact dancing in the street
musicians would be backing up news boys and gals

hat cocked to the side
screamin', *extra extra*
with rewritten headlines: Compassion Come.

It's the best gig he had in years
the trumpet player can't complain
nor can anyone cut each profane
word heard
like squeezed tube of toothpaste
is like an erupt erection
from the editorial section.

In the morning
cigarette butts are found sleeping by the band stand
while yesterday's news is caught in the grilled cheese breeze
by the family run diner
the police want to know who is responsible for this mess
for this public disturbance

We all know who
brought us together
to break the sound barrier
broadcast live from the living room kaboom
but not even the kid with two prior convictions breathes a lead
like robin hood was protected
friar tuck in a Wu-Tang Clan hoodie lights Della Fiore cathedral candles
harboring a criminal
under dark green sky
with dandelion moon
in the church basement mixing up the medicine,
signing each letter with a T.
is St. Marie

I was reading Macbeth with bad breath when I heard of the death
growing cold to an old grudge
jury and judge
worshiping the alter
of a toilet
with a bumper sticker that reads, "shit happens"
but in the guillotine suburbs

an epiphany occurred as absurd as
Gandhi doin' Murphy Brown doggy style
as the radio plays,
"hey good lookin,"
what the fuck do we have cookin'?
If we don't have the night?
If we don't push ourselves to transcend our part in it?
nothing will be
but novelist's quoting Nietzsche
spoken word means speak the fuck up
smash a wine bottle in time
send that demon back to hell
as you ride on the back of a transgendered lion
scratched up by a pterodactyl
running to a place you can call home for the night.

A lone cop gets out of a cruiser without a partner
a lone door is heard slam
people are lined up on main street
which is splattered with gig posters
as church bells ring out like the mariachi horns in Ring of Fire
I was in four feet deep
of a sleet and slush solitude
but I heard thunder crack at the exact same moment
and the sound of my shoes in the filthy snow walking back to civilization
whispering under my breath, "compassion come"
T. Paul lives
extra extra read all about it
spoken word means speak the fuck up
before death comes to us all
before we can be sainted.

Listen, on the train station sidewalk
there are two tracks
and a platform in the middle
one train carries news boys and gals who have testified every Sunday inside
the other track carries a train that is a shape shifter
turning into a number 3 bus or an ordinary car
zooming by under the exhausted evening sky

on the platform in the middle is a rockabilly poet
the host of the modern times hobo
he flashes a zippo
producing a cherry on the end of his cigarette
he was always outside smoking
St. Marie
he was always outside smoking
St. Marie
but it wasn't because he didn't want to listen
listen
that's when he talked to god.

CHAPTER TWO
THE FIRST MUSICIAN
WHO SHOUTED
"LET'S PLAY IT BY EAR"

New York Fire Escape

She says, "It's a wonderful feeling,
not wearing underwear while wearing a skirt,"
as she stands on a fire escape, one floor above street level.
I tell her, "You are like the birds at sundown,
that rest on the opposing roof top edge,
only beautiful to the pedestrians below
who take the time to look up."

Roll Over, Beethoven

Once upon a time,
I performed with a break-dancer
in the Mermaid Lounge variety show cabaret.
He wanted to perform in drag,
so we did this routine
set in a dirty seaside bar,
where he toyed and flirted with me
while I crooned like Sinatra in a three piece suit,
sitting at a shipwrecked piano
that eventually turned into a tango,
with him B-boying in four inch stiletto heels.
Never in the skit did we put out there
that he was in drag;
he was a gorgeous woman I was dancing with, period.

After the show,
Brian the stage manager said to me,
"I'm not hitting on you, C.R., but you're a very sexy man."
I was knocked out
and though I don't sleep with men,
only because the female body steals my breath like a Winnipeg winter,
it was nice to hear,
like Chuck Berry
at 4 a.m.

DOPPELGANGER

Walked by a commercial store front
under the lazy sun
on an errands-to-run afternoon,
on my way to the post modern post office,
in the drip coffee rain.

There in the display window,
was a mannequin dressed up exactly like me.
I ain't income-tax-empty-pocket-poor-artist exaggeratin',
he was my doppelganger head to toe.
Same tweed button down hat,
dark shampoo blue pin-striped vest,
lightly tinted stepped on more than once sunglasses,
and second-hand scuffed up military boots.
I gave him the finger
and mumbled "wooden piece of shit."

Tonight, under black garbage bag clouds
and the peeping tom yellow moon,
I comb through the entertainment listings
of the local free rag
to read he's been picked up for Wal-Mart's most recent
back to school campaign
and has caught the eye of an EMI rep
who just so happened
to wander by the commercial store front window
and was awestruck by his mass appeal potential.
Critics are hailing him the next big thing
and gave his newest single, "Do The Funky Mannequin" 5 stars,
from his sophomore album, Baby I Got Wood for You.

I stick my mug out the window for a refill
and stick to my guns
like a work horse of old,
and just pray my letter finds its way.

THE GOSPEL ACCORDING
TO THE PURPLE COTTON DRESS

There's girl-on-girl
and there's woman-on-woman,
according to the gospel of computer cinema.
One is two ladies tongue kissing
and playing with each other's boobs;
the other is a lady interviewing another lady about politics
or the turbulent vertigo of ladies through the ages.
I wish we could combine the two
like sewing the ripped hem of a purple cotton dress.

And of man's fetish against the invention of the wheel?
I don't really know.
But for fun, let's blame it on the French.

Tonight I feel like a boy toy
or a lazy man in Louisiana living on a swamp,
swatting flies.
My mind is some inmate's bitch.
When will I see this mademoiselle who put me through hell
 is rewriting history?
and as water falls from the theater ceiling sky,
rapidly hitting the sidewalk as we talk,
there's a rainbow in her black cherry breath.

Today was unusually balmy for this time of year;
couldn't eat,
couldn't move,
couldn't do a goddamn thing.
When will I unwrap each moment
like eternity was a masquerade ball
unrolling its tent
in the city square?
Each flash of my eyelash
a glimpse into Zora Neale Hurston's teacake recipe for manhood.

Tonight, the sounds from the main road

are the only sounds,
like waves,
like transports to heaven.
There's another
sweeping in and away
like a purple cotton dress caught on the nail of a fence post,
flapping in the awkwardly busy breeze.
Two girls are kissing in the stairwell,
turning on a woman's younger brother.
The sound from the main road is the only sound
and Romeo writes another.

Woman,
the envelope licked messiah,
the no-return-address trap door sister.

Woman,
the electric guitar
leaning against the window of the world's last great idea.

Woman,
stretched out on the bed like a wedding dress,
while lines sleep under phrases in books
that I thought were important at the time,
or more like a friend
I'd go back to once I reached the end.

Girl,
the dandelion,
the yellow flower lumped in with the weeds,
and innocence mowed down every suburban Sunday.

Girl,
the dragonfly dancer supreme.

Girl,
the scraped knee Christmas tree,
still planted in the snow-haunted woods.

Girl,
skinny in a miniskirt,

admittedly does flirt
in the palace of Joan of Arc,
light hitting metal reflecting in a gypsy's ruby pearl
between her undeveloped breast, against her fill-in-the-blank heart,
showing us where to start.

I heard Hank Williams died
in the back of a chauffeured driven Cadillac en route to a show.
"Look what a scourge is laid upon our hate that heaven finds means
    to kill our joys with love,"
wrote Shakespeare of Juliet and her Romeo.

I was just a boy on the road
to Ode to Joy.
I've been a jealous man,
a family man,
a blues man,
a Renaissance man,
and a ladies' man,
sundown
in a small village called East Van.

But I turn to the sky for consultation.
Just when I thought all sacred scripture
had all but gone and left,
but this is the Gospel according to the purple cotton dress.
As I lift up its ripped hem,
my cheek against her inner thigh,
there's a rainbow in my burnt sugar breath.

But I'm like the sounds from the main road
always drifting in and away.
Blame it on Hank Williams,
but I got them honky tonk blues.

BALLAD FOR THE STARVING ARTIST

The plane is better than the train if you want to get someplace quicker,
but on the locomotive bar car the air is filled with smoke and snicker
all because a tall middle-aged blonde and a cowboy with boots of leather
stood up passing through passengers and went into the bathroom together.
"We're not laughin' at 'em, we're laughin' with 'em," said a shit-
    faced Mr. Magic.
"We just stopped to let the freight train go by, kid, how come
    comedians are oh so tragic?"
"I don't know why this is," said the conductor who didn't drive no train,
"but let me ask you this, Mr. Magic, how come geniuses are also
    clinically insane?"
"That's a good point," said Mr. Magic as he took a sip of his drink
    from a blue plastic mug.
"On that point, kid, think of all the jazz legends that died at the
    hands of some crazy drug."
"Or the artist," continued the conductor, "who throughout her
    entire life, her work won't sell;
now it's worth millions, studied in universities, and she died
    penniless in a flea bag motel."
"Yes, life is funny," said Mr. Magic, "excuse me though kid, I need
    to top up my drink."
And with this, he left the conductor alone in the bar car to roll a
    cigarette and think.
The conductor writes a song in his head he'll forget, sings a melody
    he'll never hum again,
mumbles to himself, "Guess a motel on the Lower East Side ain't
    such a bad place for your days to end."
Blam! Blam! Two shots ring out like death metal aimed to destroy .
In the shadows stands the ladies' man, our leather-booted cowboy,
and the middle-aged blonde behind the smoke rising from the barrel
    of the gun
whispers, "Where's your poetry now, conductor, now your days on
    earth are done?"
But the conductor just laid there with a smile on his face and blood
    in his eye.
"We just gotta stop for a moment," says Mr. Magic, "let the freight
    train go by."

Suburbs of Bridge End

I told my lover
I cheated on her
so I could play a song about it.

And I wonder why
things have slipped
downhill between us,

not as far down
as a world gone wrong,
but we've definitely fallen from our utopia.
It's a hell of a song.

I'm just a coward, slow on the draw.

QUARTER PAST ELEVEN
(WE HAVE AN UNDERSTANDING)

The cat just sat on my lap,
and she's purring like Mae West
after a couple bottles of champagne.
With her tiny black paws,
she pulls out the cigarettes from my winter coat pocket,
now tobacco is dangling from her petite jaw, against her sharp teeth.
With a swift flash of her manicured claw,
she flicks the lighter,
careful not to singe her whiskers.
She's blowing smoke rings
with euphoric nostalgia of the silent film era,
while nudging me with her head to scratch behind her ear,
and ashes in my old corduroy hat.

We've come a long way in two weeks.
The first time I tried to pet her soft white belly,
she reacted like a woman being approached late at night on a badly lit
        suburban street,
or a woman being followed in an empty parking garage;
the cat fuckin' maced me.
As I held my burning eyes, keeled over on one knee,
cursing like a trucker,
I heard her run into the tiled kitchen
and the dead bolt go "click."

But now we're like Freida and Diego
in a Mexican garden full of honeysuckles and zinnias,
blessed by papaya and mango trees.
In the shadow of giant puppets to be revealed at the carnival of lost souls,
we lick salt from empty popcorn bowls
and binge on the tequila from half finished glasses
found on the kitchen counter after a swingers party.

Soon I'll be catching her alley mice and inner city birds
and she'll slip me cash.

I won't ask where it came from.
I'll just offer her a smoke
and purr.

Unicef Blues

The beach looks like a desert.
High tide, and the angry schoolboys in their uniforms
want to keep the money they've collected.
They didn't even go door to door,
but still he screams, "Give us our shiny coins!"
Their whiney revolt is pounding on my brain
like guilt should overtake me,
but when I dissect the dead frog,
I see
that the beach looks like a desert
and I've traveled to the nations of road block hunger
and kissed the wet nose of a lion deep in the jungle boogie.
Step back, schoolboys.
Don't make me say the Lord's Prayer backward with a nervous lisp,
showing you, to your horror, that it's true
what you feared all along.
God has never been anything
but a distant train whistle.

Follow that Cab

People who travel with their guitars
have an air of adventure to them,
even more than when I see someone
in a leather coat with a motorcycle helmet
under their arm.
Carrying a guitar case is almost like wearing your
heart on your sleeve,
or waving a dildo to hail a cab.

CHAPTER THREE
OUR SUN FLASHES THROUGH
THE CLOUDS LIKE A COP'S BADGE

ORPHAN

Vienna, May 7th, 1824.
Those in attendance
at the Karntnertor Theater
stood and applauded
Beethoven's 9th symphony
with a fuck protocol raucous fire storm ovation
of unbridled happiness,
though it all fell on the composer's
deaf ears.

Birds fly,
the ocean pounds the sand,
and my mother has nightmares.

Even as a kid,
from the other end of the house,
I could hear her crying in her sleep
like she was being haunted.

So I prepare my prayers,
sign the documents to make them official,
call it postmodern Joni Mitchell,
but what can you do
when even your city's subway
runs through the sky?

My mother had a baby grand.
She taught local kids how to read music
chapter by chapter.
She'd play at church,
at weddings,
or when drinking white wine with her French friend Chantelle,
who just arrived to our small Ontario town
with her two kids
from the outskirts of Montreal.
She was shacking up with our next door neighbor
who had two kids of his own,

now divorced for over a year.

Air Wolf & A-Team
were the hit shows of the day,
Madonna and George Michael
were considered risqué.
Wine glass in hand,
Chantelle loved to listen to my mother play.
Misplaced in a small town,
what can you do
when the abandoned train tracks
overrun with weeds and rust
run through the backyard?

But it broke my 9-year-old free will
when the local tough guy
showed up at our front door
lookin' for piano lessons.
He was one of the big kids,
but I knew his reputation.
My first thought as I turned down the TV
to overhear their conversation was,
I bet he wants to play in a rock & roll band.
But like the inn keeper
in us all,
my mother said, "I'm sorry, I'm all booked up."
Very gentleman-like,
not raising his voice,
he said, "Ma'am, what if I came back in a few months?"
She said, "I'm sorry," and closed the door.
In my mother's defense,
black sheep lose their beauty;
there are only so many lessons
you can give for free.

I just thought those hands
that could knock a jaw to the curb
needed a chance to touch the ivory keys
Maybe my tune would change fast
as I got older and it was my nose he was breaking in three different places

while liquored up on his dad's hidden stash
that he found in the glove box,
but then again,
maybe he'd be less likely to do so
if his hands were skilled in the art of power chords
to play under Skynyrd and Motley Crue.
But what can you do
when even limousines are being pimped out
to look like pick-up trucks?

In my mother's old age
she has built a fort in the Anglican church,
a campfire right there on the alter,
a slingshot out of a crucifix.
I think she's even stayed
in the stained glass fort overnight,
fending off her bad dreams,
conducting the crickets like her choir.

In town, I make my living
selling road maps for a nickel
to lost children in bandit rags,
standing beside a burnt down circus tent,
their wild blue eyes accentuated
by debris ash and black swan smoke, acting as warrior face paint
hidden talents in tow at the local yocal open mics
frustrated by highway detour signs:
these orphans of legitimacy
whose will has been shattered
like the shards of glass under their feet.
My mother was cut open for my birth,
then stitched back up,
has the scar to prove it
and new shoes from my sister.

My whole life
I have just craved adventure,
but tonight, fueled by chain smoking
and endless shots of Jager,
I pray my mother's nightmares stop,
for if and when they do,

world peace will kiss the belly of the church
and heaven will finally learn to sing the blues.

What else is there to do
in a ghost town,
watching as the last train pulls away?
But to open up for business:
PIANO LESSONS
FOR TOUGH GUYS
and drunk sexy women from Montreal.
I just need one student
to make it official,
call it postmodern Joni Mitchell.
The meaning of that?
Only my mother would understand.
"He really just wants
to play in a rock & roll band
with a sound so unearthly
and joyous
it could end all our nightmares."

Birds fly
the ocean pounds the sand,
and each night my mother prays
her son's music
does not fall on deaf ears.

Paris

Oh, windows, you are an interesting invention,
a square hole carved out in the middle of a cement brick wall
to see out into the world from your boxed-in painted ceiling room.

May stardust not settle on my acrylic nose
and my World War II eyes not turn sleepy.

So much to see and articulate: like tiny pipe chimneys
and an array of beige flower pots filled with hot pink petals,
faded green foreign leaves on pencil-thin stems.

I close the window's curtain before I undress
and climb into the small hotel shower.

Sorry, ladies and gay men of eternity,
but even the sun today is hidden behind the Parisian clouds.

Slow Sunday

My fingers in her wavy hair
as she goes down.
The floor begins to harden,
then up her spine,
my fist
turns into a flower garden.

Our private parts we made public,
with lips and hands
we caressed.
I fetched a bottle of white wine.
She lit two cigarettes in her mouth
like a bird building a nest.

THE CORONER'S OFFICE & FIGURE EIGHTS

My sister was a figure skater
I grew up in rinks
I know their smell well
a combination of compressed ice and popcorn.
I used to stand on a chair and draw at the counter of the little rink canteen.
I could choose one law abiding sweet treat
a Croatian chocolate bar,
bag of lick your lips salty chips
or crackerjacks with the treasure map inside
and so on and so forth.
I'd peek over the counter
talking with the nice lady who worked behind the concession,
spending hours deciding what my choice that day would be
from my bird's eye view
while I drew.

The competition side of the sport was stressful
the general bad mood if my sister didn't do well
the silence in the car driving home
the catty fights between the skaters
the Shirley Temple manager mothers always at odds
big fish in small pond coaches
and young girls in too much make-up
that I was told was so
their eyes and cheek bones could be seen from miles away

But I loved the big shows
where there were no official rules
no judging
more creative in their carnival ballet-on-ice routines
it was my introduction to show biz.

So as I stand leaning against a parking meter on Commercial,
in the back of my mind debating where to go for $3.99 breakfast
it's been a long time since I've wandered into a rink
But in between that childhood and now
I've slept in the stairwell of many a fancy hotel

made a living off of people's moonshine drape curtain desires in the
    burning forest
and notated the terrified vaudeville romance
in the Appalachian trees,
smelling the polite red tape piss aroma
of the government sanctioned sidewalks
that drowned the heaven scent of wild velvet paintings
quilted in bootlegged strip poker.
I've been called more than once to come downtown
to identify the dead body of a woman we call our city.

"Yes, it's her"
She was so disfigured
would be unrecognizable
if I hadn't known her for so long
Could be any inner city
in any 3rd world country
They pull the sheet over her face
I walk out and into the rain
and down many streets
by a river, wondering why I moved west,
where it doesn't freeze in the life of winter

One of the pictures I drew as a kid
at the canteen counter
was a woman crying.
The lady who sold the candy asked me who she was.
I replied
"The city I'll live in as a grown man."
I slid down off of my chair
and wandered into the cool rink
climbed over the boards
as Salt-n-Pepa's
"PUSH IT! PUSH IT REAL GOOD!"
pumped through the Smith Falls arena's sound system,
and I ran around the ice sliding
falling, deke'n,
in between prom queen skaters
grabbing the hand of a tall brunette,

spinning her around 'til I fell on my ass
A coach got me by the ear
led me out of the rink
into the warm waiting area
and with a look that's usually reserved
for a judge residing over a murder trial,
she demanded
"What were you thinking?!"
I replied with my hand cocked like a gun
"Just tryin' to break into show biz."

The moral of this burning question
in this endless saga
of the rich and poor debates
capitalism is the answer
except for the coroner's office
and the untold story of figure eights.

If we don't help her,
we are the shit head people
self absorbed, greedy and mean
which was written in crayon
'neath the drawing of a crying woman
who still hangs in the small rink's canteen.

SHIZER!

When I was 14,
I wanted to sing like I was 60.
Now I'm 30.
I'm halfway there.
After a concert in Frankfurt,
an old lover leaned in for a kiss.
I pulled away;
she sarcastically responded,
"Oh your lips are so rare!"
"Yeah," I replied, "like a sirloin steak, just cooked a little bit."
She frowned.
 I continued,
"Or like finding anyone other than a child with an honest smile."
She glowed then like apple juice
with a big wide-mouthed grin.
But like the boy at 14
who just discovered
the wild mercy explosion
of the Mississippi-moved to-Chicago electric wrecking ball
clanging through the big city back swamp with a growl
now in his thirties
closer yet to its imperfect pitch and uncorked moan.
At the end of the day though,
as it is with rectifying an old friendship gone astray
and a life's work on the horizon,
only halfway there.

OLD LOVE THE GAMBLER

He never exploited her sensitive skin's innocence
or cashed in on her quick cash poor choices
down hard-knock alley
intersecting with half truth's road
for the sake of a good story,
didn't sell her out to make gritty street art

But twenty years from now
he'll be rewarded
for his bloody crossroad choice
when they're both old and wrinkled
her wounds healed by gracious seashell time
his distrust disintegrated like butter left out on the kitchen counter
in mid-July.

The old man who still takes notes on the sun's shadows
will jot down a few choice crafted words
a kiss of mercy for keeping the baby messiah's whereabouts a secret
from the pit-bull authorities,
from Herod the King's trench men of horror
back in his homeless youth.

As he puts the lid back on the pen
his wife of thirty five years
will call for him at his desk
from their modest apartment's bedroom
to see if he wants to play cards or make love
before lunch.

TRUDEAU

Pierre Elliott Trudeau.
After 3 years of being Prime Minister of Canada,
he married a 22 year old
from west Vancouver
She was 30 years younger than him
and hot.

But Margaret ended up breaking Pierre's famous heart
after supposedly spending a lost weekend with Mick Jagger in New
    York City
New York has a thing with coke and Barenaked Ladies.

But Pierre, you're in my prayers
came down the parliament stairs
and your body was carried by black smoke stack train home to Montreal
to have Castro be one of your pallbearers

Pierre, I pray you're drinking red wine with Lorraine Hansberry in heaven
and she's reading you her work
never produced in her too short of a life time
Maybe she'll even pen a play
on one of your visions of a just society
and if you two kiss behind the pearly gates
I pray that bliss is a bass line
outlining the chords of a truly great man
who finally met his match

Here in eternity's hallway
I have danced the part of having a woman in every port
as ex-girlfriends plotted their revenge
in heated pool unfaithfully wounded resort
and Pierre, we can all only imagine how you felt
every time you heard the Rolling Stones on the radio
Funny, but he is not alone in this
we have all sat on both sides of this eternal hallway
And for the man who is famous for the line:
"The state has no place in the bedrooms of this nation"

we didn't exactly repay the favor
when his marriage broke up.

We have wasted so much time
over a Bill Clinton blow job
do you know what Trudeau would've said
if he'd been caught doing a line of coke
and getting head in the oval office?
"Just watch me."

This is not a gossip column
I don't care if Margaret slept with
Mick Jagger,
Keith Richards,
Robert Plant or Jimmy Page
and this is not a put down
to any man
dating a woman half his age.
This is about a woman with sapphire eyes
and Ruby Tuesday cheeks
and about every man that shuts the fuck up
and listen's when there woman speaks

Say what you want about Pierre Elliott Trudeau
but he stood up to America
and no other Prime Minister
before or since
has done that
except maybe Diefenbaker during the bay of pigs
as John F. Kennedy took extra spoiled rich kid swigs of scotch
        fuddle duddle beotch
and Trudeau, with more then a bag of bilingual tricks,
returned the sentiment while in Cuba in '76
"Viva Cuba y el pueblo cubano¡ Viva el Primer Ministro Fidel Castro¡
 Viva la amistad cubano-canadiens¡"

Like a referee callin' the fight in the 9th round from the ring
Pierre pulled out Canadian peace keepers
from Vietnam
which gained him the highest honor in the world

to have Richard Nixon call him a "fuckin' asshole"
on the Watergate tapes.
Which makes me think,
will we ever have a Prime Minister
rise up and lead us the same way again?
His response to the impeached president
"I've been called worse, by better men."

We are not just the polite nation
beside the super power they try to pin on us
Sorry.
We were the Underground Railroad's destination
from slavery.
We were the oasis for draft dodgers
seeking refuge from the U.S. military.
We were the 3rd country in the world
to recognize same sex marriage
This is our history
this is our fuck you
they like us in Europe.

But my dear friends
we are losing our Character
like a Shakespearian actor
now in a bunny outfit doing TV shampoo commercials
Oh the winds of change have blown
It's not a dispute who in a suit looks sharper,
but now America has Barack Obama
and we're left with Steven Harper.

It's war
We are just a small fraction
of what we once stood for
That's why
a 22-year-old American soldier
can show up in Thunderbay, Ontario
seeking refugee status
and can be sent back by the Canadian government
to serve 15 months in U.S. military prison
The train don't stop here no more.

We need another
Pierre Elliott Trudeau.

SERVANTS' QUARTERS

I sleep in the servants' quarters
naked woman beside me in bed
my quarrel lies not with being pressed by reporters,
my fight tonight was to write what you've just read.

On the 3rd floor of the mansion inn,
she brews coffee and pours me a cup.
Dull razor against my skin
in the shared bathroom I shave and clean up.

The stairs down are many in number,
I smoke 'neath the willow tree.
One like it was used for lumber
to house the travelers in room 303.

Tonight I study the art of sorrow,
how the mirror can be an unmarked tomb.
By this time tomorrow,
we'll be stayin' in the comrades of the resistance spare bedroom.

Tomorrow we check out at 11:30.
If the maid's late we'll stay a little longer I suppose.
My answering machine records a hurdy gurdy
and a message from a country singer in town for a string of shows.

On the TV I listened to another man's prayers,
laughed aloud and cried amen
one more time I descend down the stairs
to smoke 'neath the tree in the rain at 2 am.

I sleep in the servants' quarters,
naked woman beside me in bed
my quarrel lies not with being pressed by reporters,
my fight tonight was to write what you've just read.

POCKET KNIFE

On my daughter's fifth birthday
I got her a dollhouse and a pocketknife.
She keeps the dollhouse in her room with her other toys
but the knife stays in her pocket
each time she leaves the house.

I told her,
"If any man ever tries to make you touch his penis
chop it the fuck off."
This is not an act of violence,
this is feminism at its finest
and,
"if any man ever tries to touch your vagina,
slash his fingers and shove them down his throat."
This is not over doing it,
this is revolution in its final hour.

I gave her the dollhouse
on the 17th of February.
she was born on the 11th.
I was on the road,
but on my return
found a saved piece of birthday cake in the fridge
and a little girl excited
to show me the parcels
that had already arrived in the mail.

So before I set out again
with my pocket harmonica
a.k.a. the blues harp,
I had a talk with her
about the evils that exist
so her wits would be razor sharp.
"Some adults are sick in the head," I said,
as I stood in the bathroom shaving.
When she inquired what I meant, I said,
"You know when your stomach has a belly ache

if anyone touches you in a way that doesn't feel right, it's wrong,
and I don't care who they are
or what they say will happen if you tell anyone,
you come and tell your mommy and me right away."
She said, "I will come and tell you and mommy right away."
She really liked that part
that, yeah, big people couldn't always tell her what to do.

But I'm always leaving.
Ask anybody who tried to get a little bit close to me
those who tried to
HOUSE TRAIN GRAFFITI,
while deep down,
they know I belong
with the tracks and wild flowers.

That's why my love life is like a car wreck on the side of the road
pedestrians walkin' and cars driving by
with their red eyes glaring
in the black of night.
They see the body pile up,
the lights flashing,
they know its gonna be gruesome,
but they can't resist to sneak a peek
to see who's been killed by curiosity.
I'm a paramedic on the scene
in my 1986 shocking pink,
laying beside a woman
with a gash on her forehead
from trying to hold onto something she thought was beautiful,
but it was lover
after lover
after lover
each one would confess
how they were molested at some point as a kid.
And I would close their eyes
when the spirit left them
and drive away in an ambulance
with no siren blaring,
but with the window down

and the radio up.
In the shotgun seat
a 5 year old
who says,
"The rhymes don't always have to make sense, Dad,
just like Dr. Suess,"
but I'm haunted by the darkness,
knowing that 98 percent of those in the sex trade
suffered as kids from sexual abuse.
I want to cut out your fucking tongue
I'm going to slice out my own
if none of us can remember the song
that's gonna save kids from this fate
if you remember just a gist of how that song goes ?
I will put my hand on your cheek
and kiss you so soft and gentle and deep
and as our eyes open at the same time,
I will whisper,
"Revolution in its final hour."

On my daughter's fifth birthday,
I got her a dollhouse and a pocketknife.
She keeps the dollhouse in her room with her other toys,
but the knife stays in her pocket
each time she leaves the house.
She's just a kid
with her wits about her
feminism at its finest.

CHAPTER FOUR
A DRAGON, WITH HIS TAIL
CURLED UP LIKE A GARDEN HOSE

Oakland Garage Band

They say people look like their pets,
or that they are an extension of their owner's personality.
Well, same goes for people sitting behind their crafts
at a flea market.
There were no dreadlocked Rastas selling vintage Metallica t-shirts
and bedroom-wall-sized posters of Def Leppard.

And there were no 40-something
greasy-haired Kevin Smith look-a-likes
who still live with their mothers
selling
hand-carved
wooden
African statues and djembes,
which would've been somewhat eye-opening amazing,
like a lady licking a lollipop
or Ray Charles in a low demon baritone
like a wounded wolf whispering, "Ring of Fire,"
his throat smoldering like campfire coals.

My eye caught by bar star sex novelty toys,
keyboards from the 80's,
prescription sunglasses,
a Bruce Springsteen drag queen photo book,
and the smell from the Mexican cantina.

Maybe I'll get a pet bird for my shoulder.
As I sit beside my retail price merchandise after a show,
the parrot can go,
"auk, ten dollars."
That would be funny,
like ice cream on an elephant's penis
in a documentary
aired on PBS during a fundraising drive.

Tonight,
the giant door
to the poker playin' night is locked down

as we sleep in a garage in Oakland,
resting like a 1969 Plymouth convertible with the headlights left on
so she can see without the spotlight in the sky.

In the dark, dogs bark
and my lover reads Catcher in the Rye.

GREETINGS FROM ACROSS THE OCEAN

Faded bikini,
Seattle warm water,
unclouded moon evening.

My shy lover naked beside you,
with smooth stone flesh,
a bird of paradise ducking in for a splash bath.

Us in that big double bed
that took up almost the entire floor space of the musty room,
the beautiful woman intelligent as an old gray owl
is touching your back, letting out alpha female soft coo's and moans,
but feeling the panic of her man pushing for a three-way on her one
    lane street.

The lady's touch is then joined by a male piano player's right hand
grasping new surface.
Yes, this one,
with the fingertips rough around the edges,
glides
up
from your spine
and over
to your bare breast,
curling the nipple with index finger like putting a filter in a joint of hash.
The woman in the middle softly whispers a gasp, "Has he gone too far?"
But you turn around.
Now your cream back is against the unwashed sheets,
and their easily forgettable pattern.
Your breasts are in view.
With soulful big eyes of an ancient heroine long-lost in modern times,
a sigh of relief,

her
man
hasn't
pushed the zebra into extinction.

The lady leans in and kisses you on your round lips,
which later she talks of with joyous eyelash remembrance—
that's what she liked the most,
your big, soft monsoon lips.

As the man sucks now on your pink nipples, swallowing saliva
to end the longing exile
anticipated fantasy,
finally breathing real breath,
like New York in the spring time.

For the next six hours 'til the morning's light came
through the closed window's ratty curtain,
the three of us made love,
only stopping to giggle and smoke
and the tension was gone,
sincerely evaporated.
We felt like teenagers getting away with a police chase joyride,
doing something not talked about in home-ec
or on sitcoms,
just maybe in the Old Testament.

When sleep finally overtook us,
our bodies happily entwined like mud-soaked branches of
a well-rooted young tree,
us three.

I still see you in fresh dark blue Americana night
in your faded bikini,
in warm water
with colored lights.

My rough fingers wish to undo the string from behind,
gently sliding my palm up your wet back
to the loosely-tied knot,

slowly watching it glide down your shoulders
while the short-haired Queen of the Nile's hand,
gracefully underwater,
slips in your swimsuit bottoms,
making you close your eyes
and explicitly smile.

Her cheek
against your shoulder.
My lips everywhere at once.
Hope you are well.

Greetings from across the ocean.

Destiny and the Green Grass of Flagstaff

o.k here we go
in a run down
red shit box
that had to be jumper cabled back to life
at the last fuel station
as other cars whiz by
at razor sharp speed,
we're just happy to be in the game.

It's warmer at dark
than it's been all day.
I'm still horny as a 15-year-old boy,
but now I can do something about it.

Gotta learn to outlaw love
and kiss the rust
of the sleeping German woman
in the back seat.
I will sniff her essence like a bar of mechanic's soap.
She's been my best kept secret
and my out in the open arms dealer
in this ho-hum world of broken robots,
her flesh and fire has outrun them all.

Here we go
like hard rain
driving through the desert
on the wings of no censorship.
No blank checks,
just the day to day hell to pay
from living out of your suitcase
in a freedom whirlwind experiment.
All thanks to a 15-year-old
who still sits at the helm
of this fearless dream
the great American voyage of vagabond black magic,
guarding the vision ferociously

and in charge
of my old man soul's entry to Leadbelly heaven.

OPEN LETTER TO A BEAUTIFUL 20 YEAR OLD

I liked you best in jeans and ball cap
I fell in love with you in a tank top and work pants,
hair pulled back, nothing fancy
at 10:15 p.m

On our first date,
you wore a light blue bra
under a loose translucent white shirt.
When you greeted me at the downstairs door,
I wondered why you were having me over:
you so stunning and me so shady
with a 5 o'clock shadow.

Our first public outing,
we met at a main street bar.
I watched from the sidewalk
as you got out of the cab like it was a yellow dressing room,
the street's busy intersection, your runway
heels, long coat, make-up under your blue eyes,
at first I wondered,
Where's the girl in the tank top?
when you appeared through traffic
dressed to the 9's.

When we were first lovers,
I loved how you looked in your pawnshop nightie
or other inexpensive lingerie,
my pockets crammed with other women's phone numbers and addresses
and you coming home in a pretty dress,
proclaiming you weren't wearing any underwear.
As time pressed on,
that turned into big sweaters
and jogging pants,
and I became more and more all yours,
hangin' out in that downtown apartment,
lighting tobacco reefer
at 4:20.

But my favorite outfit of yours was coming home to find you, the artist.
loud spoken music,
broken glass,
Black tar on your hands and face, trying to SMASH
thick Wine BOTTLES wrapped in towels,
so outstandingly beautiful in your solitaire creativity.
Puzzle without pieces,
Monet muzzle unmuted mosaic
at an ungodly hour.

The artist up to her armpits
in past midnight projects,
with haiku vision and voodoo precision,
while uncle Charlie's RECORDED monotone voice explains from
    your tiny computer speakers:
WRITING POETRY IS LIKE TAKING A GOOD BEER SHIT
Nothing fancy.
I might have removed my shirt
and looked at the clock on the stove or the microwave
to notate the exact time of this moment
I was so happy.

It's now 6:55 on the east coast of Canada,
so its 3:55 out west.
This Halloween, let's dress up as each other.
As always, you can wear what you'd like,
but I'm wearing jeans and a ball cap.

A Town in Eastern Ontario

The wind is speed reader
it's violently flipping through the glossy pages
of the magazine's ripped manuscript,
absorbing its wet words
like a dry humored sponge.
The sheet music, with shaky handwritten scribbles of melody and tempo
(notated in smoker's cough and small miracles)
is face down in a toilet,
while the Roman Catholic soul
of the slain singer
floats in the bird feeder,
killing any hope
of tropical rain.

Into the bar room drifts a mischievous breeze,
while the underage son of pathos
is seen in the back corner
thumbing through a dime store paperback novel,
leaning against an old jukebox.
It reads,
"Like the fox I run with the hunted
and if I'm not the happiest man on earth,
I'm surely the luckiest man alive."

In the cherry blossom graveyard,
wind chimes find the blues scale
with the few notes they've been bestowed
the patient boy is found
renewing his vows
like an archeologist
in a sandstorm,
following a northern star
while it snows.

On this cold highway town morning,
"let sleeping dogs lie," the inscription suggests
as birds chirp on a headstone of gray
But born leader,

the wind is a speed reader
look, it's flipping through a book
on a perfect windy day.

13 Station Road, a 12 Bar Blues

Last night dreamt
of the windy grass
in and amongst the rock and armored thorn,
on the ever so important
and not so distant hill
behind the childhood house I was born.

The apple trees were God's nose hair,
us kids climbing giant pine sap covered staircases
in front of
13 Station Road.

Old brush forts,
green lawns being mowed
or watered in the nearby
neighborhood distance,
and black to locals
was the color of night.
My sugar mountain was
13 Station Road:

the highway at the bottom of our street
that would take me to Ottawa or Kingston,
and in returning,
the long walk past all the sleeping houses
with closed curtains,
locked windows.
This was my funeral procession with no pallbearers
up to
13 Station Road.

The sun is orange bright today in Piccadilly circus.
I'll wear Kevin Bacon sunglasses
and take a stroll through the pizzazz of the theater district
and up red light sanctioned back alleys.

Last night dreamt

of the windy grass
in and amongst the rock and armored thorn,
on the ever so important
and not so distant hill
beside the childhood house I was born.

LITTLE ANGEL ON THE TOILET

Your neighbor
comes knocking
with a gun in her sweaty palm,
but you are remarkably calm,
like the clean slate morning
before the blind date night.
Miss Miller is a killer
she's trying to take a dump on your parade.
But you can't control the world,
just your own worried garbage soul.

Kiss the dead bird of your brain
as you sit behind the locked stall door
in the restroom
of a country bar.
It's kinda like what Chris Rock once said:
"You keep shittin' cause I ain't quittin'."

SECRET MISSION

When I was a kid, I wanted to change my name to MC Howling Wolf
and D.J. Muddy Waters.
I was memorizing the dirty words of Ice-T
while simulating the harmonica sound
of Sonny Boy Williamson,
but deep down
I wanted to smell the gray area armpit of rock and roll,
'cause the bakery on Venables and Commercial just wasn't doin' it,
even at 5 a.m.
when the oven's aroma would entwine with the wind
at still-black early morn.
I wanted to stand on fuck-genocide-don't-be-denied sidewalks
and listen to the history lessons I missed in high school,
but deep down I wanted to see some ghosts
or at least feel the antique rhythms of streets
where modern messiahs had actually walked
with blood in their fingernails
and stern brows like comic super heroes
who left home to roam
on some type of secret mission.

HARLEM 1964
There's a D.J. in the corner
in tinted sunglasses.
He's somewhat bored or somewhat stoned.
Plays only the hits of Motown.
Those in attendance are mostly men.
It's mostly empty.
Just that 4 in the afternoon, moderately dangerous type of crowd.
The bartender's got blue slacks,
a purple shirt,
a loose chain,
a towel chasing the sweat from his brown brow,
and a toothpick resting on his bottom lip
pointing down,
it stands erect

and ripples in his ebony forehead
as a holy fuck flamboyant black man
walks into the club with a guitar in his hand
with a record between his ribcage and his elbow.
He looks like an avant-garde pimp,
a beautiful black hippie with a feather in his hat to boot,
but like a machine gun,
he beelines it from the front door to the D.J.
The bartender out of earshot range
watches as the just-out-of-the-army rebelling hoodlum
hands the record to the D.J.
and the D.J. puts it on the free turn table.
This musical outlaw seeming pleased,
sets down his guitar and lights a cigarette
as "I Heard It Through the Grapevine" fades to its close.
Through the whole Harlem club sound system blares . . .
"How many roads must a man walk down
before you call him a man?
Yes and how many seas must the white dove sail
before she sleeps in the sand?
Yes and how many. . . "
"Turn that goddamn wannabe blues man cocksucker off! This ain't a
    folk club motherfucker!"
pipes the bartender, who is also the owner,
so the D.J. makes the fast switch.

THE OWNER OF THE RECORD
has his elbows on his knees
and his head in his hands,
snaps out of it,
splashes a grin,
grabs the record
and heads to the light outside the disco.
The bartender stops him.
"What was you thinkin', son? Comin' in here dressed up
like a hippie, playin' hillbilly music.
You just tryin' to rile us up?"
"No," said the musical outlaw, not missing a beat,
"just wanted to hear the song is all."

And with that, the light hits his gypsy half-Cherokee face
out to the street,
fruit stands,
the smell of urban delicacies,
people walking up and down,
left and right.
A woman approaches him.
"Jimmy, where the fuck have you been?"
"I'm sorry, baby, but I. . . ."
"Don't 'sorry' me, I should rip out your appendix,
Mr. Blue Flames Jimi fuckin' Hendrix.
I went in to buy a pack of smokes, when I came out, you'd vanished
     into thin air!"
He instantly kisses the woman.
She shoots a look back like,
"You're going to have to earn my forgiveness."
They walk home with her shoulders under the love of his arm
and her hair against his red and brown watercolor neck,
as the wind cries Mary through the flowers in the urban windowsills,
that if you put your nose to,
smell like shampoo in a child's freshly washed head of hair.

HE WAS THE WORLD'S GREATEST GUITAR PLAYER
who loved the songs of Bob Dylan,
and to this day
we will mock both of their voices
'cause neither could sing that uptown soul.
People ask, "So you're like some kinda beat-box blues poet?"
No.
This is the gray area of rock and roll.
I changed my name
to D.J Don't Be Denied
and off I ran.
How many roads must a man walk down
before you'll call him a man?
'Cause kid,
I got blood in my fingernails
and a stern brow
like a comic super hero

who left home to roam
on some type of secret mission

and the wind began to howl.

IF ONLY SHAKESPEARE COULD SING

She said, "You love music more than you love me,"
then climbed onto the big yellow school bus,
the shy brave stranger,
wanting to hide from the staring eyes of the other kids already aboard.
It was meant to break to my heart,
and it did.

Smart kid.

At 25 I had become a man with troubles so big and heavy that they
        outweighed execution.
And now this final blow
of another unsuccessful father having to leave his daughter
with his parents
and go out into the world and work.
That morning,
I left this place of sad dialogue and unfixable sorrow

traveled west.
Then to Britain and its pints of Guy Fawkes fireworks,
Switzerland and its dead-eye audience,
Chicago and its white kid hip-hop,
Montreal's frozen folk singers.
Barrier breaker moment:
eye contact was made
as native elders in a pow wow chanted and droned on drums,
which climaxed with them singin' the fine young cannibals like no one else.
Seattle's shotgun suicide with no stunt double but able blackouts
and the trickery of a fake hundred dollar bill for a ten dollar's purchase,
Eugene's back seat momma college gig mayhem,
San Fransisco's Fillmore bonfire, the ashes of epitaph
and the Los Angeles lion hunt
along side Neil Young's niece.
Finally setting down my musical axe
in a city thick with roots of my adult life entangled in its vines.

At my lover's apartment off of Davie,

the sun beamed into the room like a flashlight in a graveyard
trying to find a name on a headstone.
Writing in my little notebook
while lying on her white carpeted living room floor
stained with red wine, covered with baking soda
in the early afternoon.
She asked, "What are you writing?"
I replied, "My daughter arrives in two days, my parents are bringing
    her home."
"Are you writing her a poem?"
"No, a song."

New Write Bloody Books for 2012

Strange Light
The *New York Times* says, "There's something that happens when you read Derrick Brown, a rekindling of faith in the weird, hilarious, shocking, beautiful power of words." This is the final collection from Derrick Brown, one of America's top-selling and touring poets. Everything hilarious and stirring is illuminated. The power of *Strange Light* is waiting.

Who Farted Wrong? Illustrated Weight Loss For the Mind
Syd Butler (of the sweet band, Les Savvy Fav) creates sketchy morsels to whet your appetite for wrong, and it will be delicious. There is no need to read between the lines of this new style of flash thinking speed illustration in this hilarious new book. Why? There are not that many lines.

New Shoes on a Dead Horse
The Romans believed that an artist's inspiration came from a spirit, called a genius, that lived in the walls of the artist's home. This character appears throughout Sierra DeMulder's book, providing charming commentary and biting insight on the young author's creative process and emotional path.

Good Grief
Elegantly-wrought misadventures as a freshly-graduated Michigan transplant, Stevie Edwards stumbles over foal legs through Chicago and kneels down to confront the wreckage of her skinned knees.

After the Witch Hunt
Megan Falley showcases her fresh, lucid poetry with a refreshing lack of jaded undertones. Armed with both humor and a brazen darkness, each poem in this book is another swing of the pick axe in this young woman's tunnel, insistent upon light.

I Love Science!
Humorous and thought provoking, Shanney Jean Maney's book effortlessly combines subjects that have previously been thought too diverse to have anything in common. Science, poetry and Jeff Goldblum form covalent bonds that put the poetic fire underneath our bunsen burners. A Lab Tech of words, Maney turns language into curious, knowledge-hungry poetry. Foreword by Lynda Barry.

Time Bomb Snooze Alarm
Bucky Sinister, a veteran poet of the working class, layers his gritty truths with street punk humor. A menagerie of strange people and stranger moments that linger in the dark hallway of Sinister's life. Foreword by Randy Blythe of "Lamb of God".

News Clips and Ego Trips
A collection of helpful articles from *Next...* magazine, which gave birth to the Southern California and national poetry scene in the mid-'90s. It covers the growth of spoken word, page poetry and slam, with interviews and profiles of many poets and literary giants like Patricia Smith, Henry Rollins and Miranda July. Edited by G. Murray Thomas.

Slow Dance With Sasquatch
Jeremy Radin invites you into his private ballroom for a waltz through the forest at the center of life, where loneliness and longing seamlessly shift into imagination and humor.

The Smell of Good Mud
Queer parenting in conservative Oklahoma, Lauren Zuniga finds humor and beauty in this collection of new poems. This explores the grit and splendor of collective living, and other radical choices. It is a field guide to blisters and curtsies.

OTHER WRITE BLOODY BOOKS (2003 - 2011)

Birthday Girl with Possum (2011)
Brendan Constantine's second book of poetry examines the invisible lines
between wonder & disappointment, ecstasy & crime, savagery & innocence.

The Bones Below (2010)
National Slam Champion Sierra DeMulder performs and teaches
with the release of her first book of hard-hitting, haunting poetry.

The Constant Velocity of Trains (2008)
The brain's left and right hemispheres collide in Lea Deschenes' Pushcart-Nominated
book of poetry about physics, relationships, and life's balancing acts.

Heavy Lead Birdsong (2008)
Award-winning academic poet Ryler Dustin releases his most
definitive collection of surreal love poetry.

Uncontrolled Experiments in Freedom (2008)
Boston underground art scene fixture Brian Ellis
becomes one of America's foremost narrative poetry performers.

Yesterday Won't Goodbye (2011)
Boston gutter punk Brian Ellis releases his second book of poetry,
filled with unbridled energy and vitality.

Write About an Empty Birdcage (2011)
Debut collection of poetry from Elaina M. Ellis that flirts with loss,
reveres appetite, and unzips identity.

Ceremony for the Choking Ghost (2010)
Slam legend Karen Finneyfrock's second book of poems ventures
into the humor and madness that surrounds familial loss.

Pole Dancing to Gospel Hymns (2008)
Andrea Gibson, a queer, award-winning poet who tours with Ani DiFranco,
releases a book of haunting, bold, nothing-but-the-truth ma'am poetry.

These Are the Breaks (2011)
Essays from one of hip-hops deftest public intellectuals, Idris Goodwin

Bring Down the Chandeliers (2011)
Tara Hardy, a working-class queer survivor of incest, turns sex,
trauma and forgiveness inside out in this collection of new poems.

City of Insomnia (2008)
Victor D. Infante's noir-like exploration of unsentimental truth and poetic exorcism.

The Last Time as We Are (2009)
A new collection of poems from Taylor Mali, the author
of "What Teachers Make," the most forwarded poem in the world.

In Search of Midnight: the Mike Mcgee Handbook of Awesome (2009)
Slam's geek champion/class clown Mike McGee on his search for midnight
through hilarious prose, poetry, anecdotes, and how-to lists.

1,000 Black Umbrellas (2011)
Daniel McGinn's first internationally released collection from 'everyone's favorite
unknown author' sings from the guts with the old school power of poetry.

Over the Anvil We Stretch (2008)
2-time poetry slam champ Anis Mojgani's first collection: a Pushcart-Nominated
batch of backwood poetics, Southern myth, and rich imagery.

The Feather Room (2011)
Anis Mojgani's second collection of poetry explores storytelling and
poetic form while traveling farther down the path of magic realism.

Animal Ballistics (2009)
Trading addiction and grief for empowerment and humor with her poetry,
Sarah Morgan does it best.

Rise of the Trust Fall (2010)
Award-winning feminist poet Mindy Nettifee
releases her second book of funny, daring, gorgeous, accessible poems.

Love in a Time of Robot Apocalypse (2011)
Latino-American poet David Perez releases his first book
of incisive, arresting, and end-of-the-world-as-we-know-it poetry.

No More Poems About the Moon (2008)
A pixilated, poetic and joyful view of a hyper-sexualized,
wholeheartedly confused, weird, and wild America with Michael Roberts.

The New Clean (2011)
Jon Sands' poetry redefines what it means to laugh, cry, mop it up and start again.

Miles of Hallelujah (2010)
Slam poet/pop-culture enthusiast Rob "Ratpack Slim" Sturma
shows first collection of quirky, fantastic, romantic poetry.

Sunset at the Temple of Olives (2011)
Paul Suntup's unforgettable voice merges subversive surrealism
and vivid grief in this debut collection of poetry.

Spiking the Sucker Punch (2009)
Nerd heartthrob, award-winning artist and performance poet,
Robbie Q. Telfer stabs your sensitive parts with his wit-dagger.

Racing Hummingbirds (2010)
Poet/performer Jeanann Verlee releases an award-winning book
of expertly crafted, startlingly honest, skin-kicking poems.

Live for a Living (2007)
Acclaimed performance poet Buddy Wakefield releases his second collection
about healing and charging into life face first.

Gentleman Practice (2011)
Righteous Babe Records artist and 3-time International Poetry Champ
Buddy Wakefield spins a nonfiction tale of a relay race to the light.

How to Seduce a White Boy in Ten Easy Steps (2011)
Debut collection for feminist, biracial poet Laura Yes Yes
dazzles with its explorations into the politics and metaphysics of identity.

WRITE BLOODY ANTHOLOGIES

The Elephant Engine High Dive Revival (2009)
Our largest tour anthology ever! Features unpublished work by
Buddy Wakefield, Derrick Brown, Anis Mojgani and Shira Erlichman!

The Good Things About America (2009)
American poets team up with illustrators to recognize the beauty and wonder in our
nation. Various authors. Edited by Kevin Staniec and Derrick Brown

Junkyard Ghost Revival (2008)
Tour anthology of poets, teaming up for a journey of the US in a small van.
Heart-charging, socially active verse.

The Last American Valentine:
Illustrated Poems To Seduce And Destroy (2008)
Acclaimed authors including Jack Hirschman, Beau Sia, Jeffrey McDaniel,
Michael McClure, Mindy Nettifee and more. 24 authors and 12 illustrators
team up for a collection of non-sappy love poetry. Edited by Derrick Brown

Learn Then Burn (2010)
Exciting classroom-ready anthology for introducing new writers
to the powerful world of poetry. Edited by Tim Stafford and Derrick Brown.

Learn Then Burn Teacher's Manual (2010)
Tim Stafford and Molly Meacham's turn key classroom-safe guide
to accompany *Learn Then Burn*: A modern poetry anthology for the classroom.

Knocking at the Door: Poems for Approaching the Other (2011)
An exciting compilation of diverse authors that explores the concept of the Other
from all angles. Innovative writing from emerging and established poets.

WRITEBLOODY
QUALITY AMERICAN BOOKS

WWW.WRITEBLOODY.COM

PULL YOUR BOOKS UP
BY THEIR BOOTSTRAPS

Write Bloody Publishing distributes and promotes great books of fiction, poetry and art every year. We are an independent press dedicated to quality literature and book design, with an office in Long Beach, CA.

Our employees are authors and artists so we call ourselves a family. Our design team comes from all over America: modern painters, photographers and rock album designers create book covers we're proud to be judged by.

We publish and promote 8-12 tour-savvy authors per year. We are grass-roots, D.I.Y., bootstrap believers. Pull up a good book and join the family. Support independent authors, artists and presses.

Visit us online:

WRITEBLOODY.COM

CPSIA information can be obtained at www.ICGtesting.com
Printed in the USA
LVOW111742210212

269778LV00002B/3/P